D0852723

To: Mrs. McNish

From
SHANE

Mrs Aulissh
SHANE

Those Who Care Teach

Written and compiled by Sarah M. Hupp

Illustrated by Charles Waller

Designed by Arlene Greco

Inspire Books is an imprint of
Peter Pauper Press, Inc.

For permissions please see the
last page of this book.

Text copyright © 1999
Peter Pauper Press, Inc.
202 Mamaroneck Avenue
White Plains, NY 10601
Illustrations copyright © 1994
Peter Pauper Press, Inc.
All rights reserved
ISBN 0-88088-129-1
Printed in China
11 10 9 8 7 6 5

Visit us at www.peterpauper.com

Those Who Care Teach

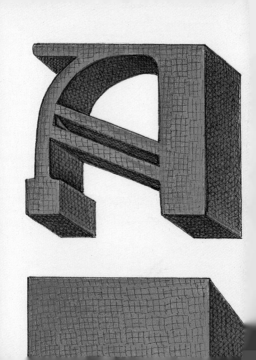

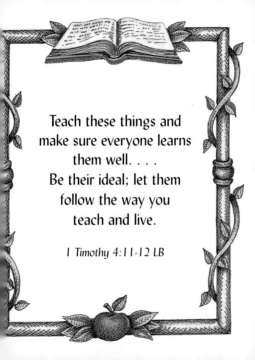

Teach these things and
make sure everyone learns
them well. . . .
Be their ideal; let them
follow the way you
teach and live.

1 Timothy 4:11-12 LB

Only when we have
knelt before God
and learned can
we stand before
students and teach.

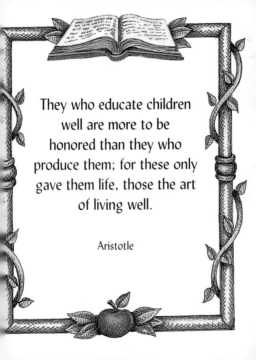

They who educate children well are more to be honored than they who produce them; for these only gave them life, those the art of living well.

Aristotle

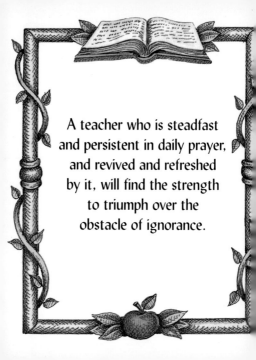

A teacher who is steadfast
and persistent in daily prayer,
and revived and refreshed
by it, will find the strength
to triumph over the
obstacle of ignorance.

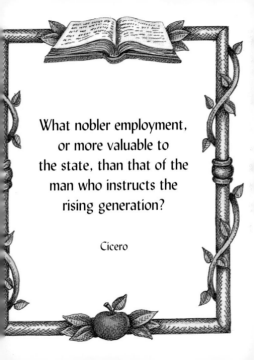

What nobler employment,
or more valuable to
the state, than that of the
man who instructs the
rising generation?

Cicero

Don't ask God to give you good students; ask instead that He will give you students who will see His goodness in you.

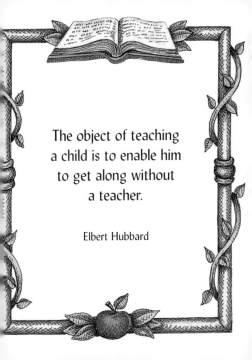

The object of teaching
a child is to enable him
to get along without
a teacher.

Elbert Hubbard

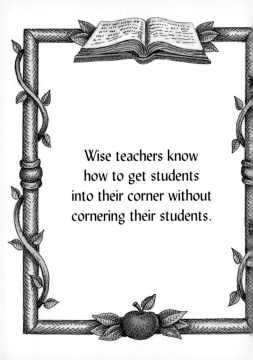

Wise teachers know
how to get students
into their corner without
cornering their students.

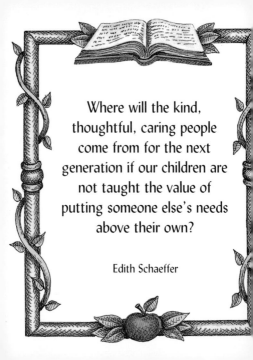

Where will the kind, thoughtful, caring people come from for the next generation if our children are not taught the value of putting someone else's needs above their own?

Edith Schaeffer

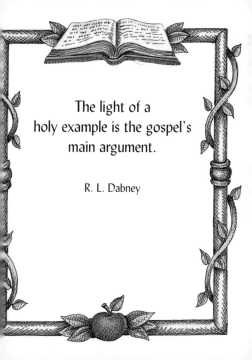

The light of a
holy example is the gospel's
main argument.

R. L. Dabney

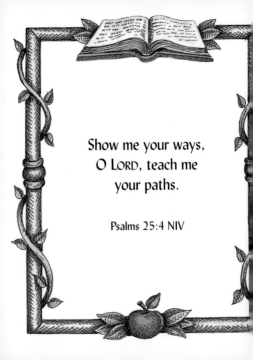

Show me your ways,
O LORD, teach me
your paths.

Psalms 25:4 NIV

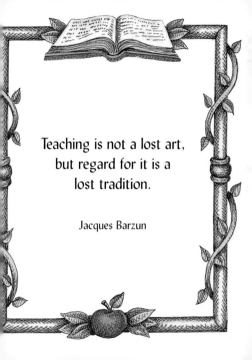

Teaching is not a lost art,
but regard for it is a
lost tradition.

Jacques Barzun

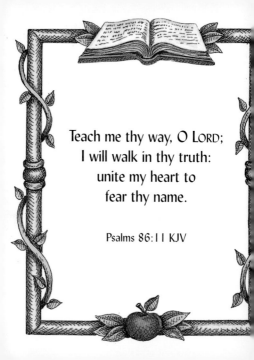

Teach me thy way, O LORD;
I will walk in thy truth:
unite my heart to
fear thy name.

Psalms 86:11 KJV

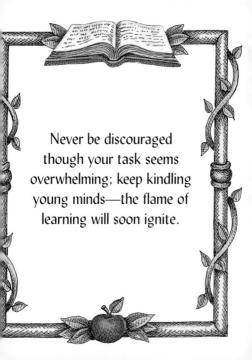

Never be discouraged
though your task seems
overwhelming; keep kindling
young minds—the flame of
learning will soon ignite.

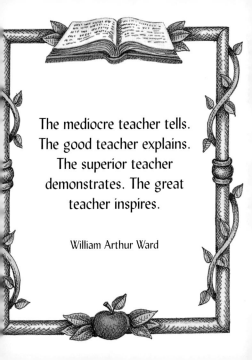

The mediocre teacher tells.
The good teacher explains.
The superior teacher
demonstrates. The great
teacher inspires.

William Arthur Ward

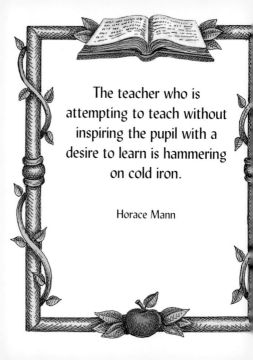

The teacher who is attempting to teach without inspiring the pupil with a desire to learn is hammering on cold iron.

Horace Mann

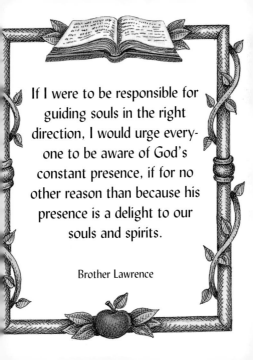

If I were to be responsible for guiding souls in the right direction, I would urge everyone to be aware of God's constant presence, if for no other reason than because his presence is a delight to our souls and spirits.

Brother Lawrence

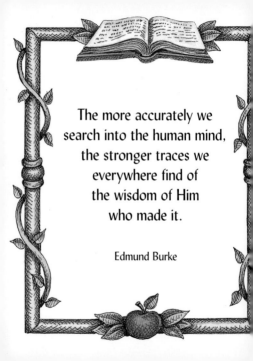

The more accurately we
search into the human mind,
the stronger traces we
everywhere find of
the wisdom of Him
who made it.

Edmund Burke

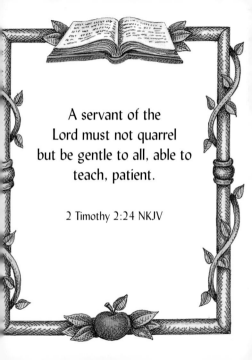

A servant of the
Lord must not quarrel
but be gentle to all, able to
teach, patient.

2 Timothy 2:24 NKJV

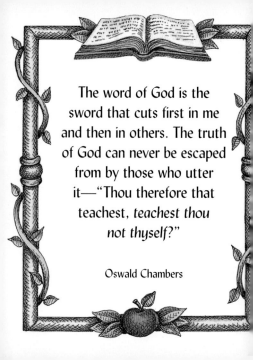

The word of God is the
sword that cuts first in me
and then in others. The truth
of God can never be escaped
from by those who utter
it—"Thou therefore that
teachest, *teachest thou
not thyself?*"

Oswald Chambers

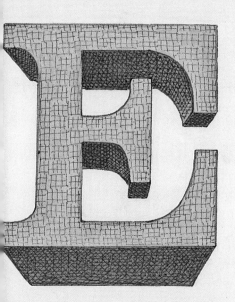

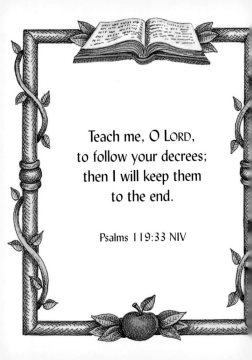

Teach me, O LORD,
to follow your decrees;
then I will keep them
to the end.

Psalms 119:33 NIV

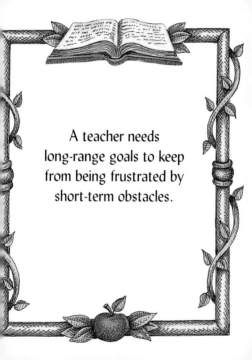

A teacher needs long-range goals to keep from being frustrated by short-term obstacles.

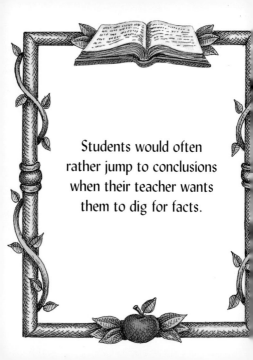

Students would often rather jump to conclusions when their teacher wants them to dig for facts.

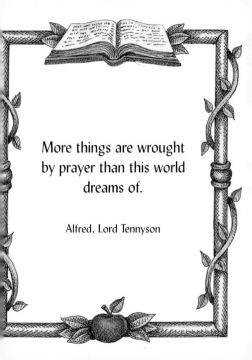

More things are wrought
by prayer than this world
dreams of.

Alfred, Lord Tennyson

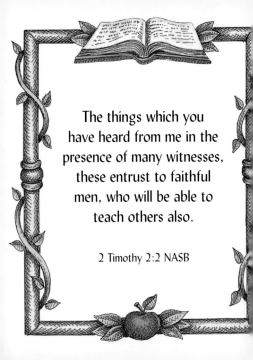

The things which you have heard from me in the presence of many witnesses, these entrust to faithful men, who will be able to teach others also.

2 Timothy 2:2 NASB

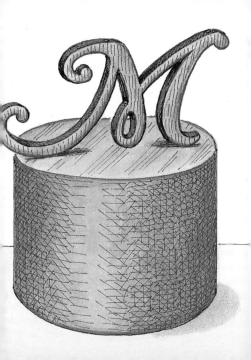

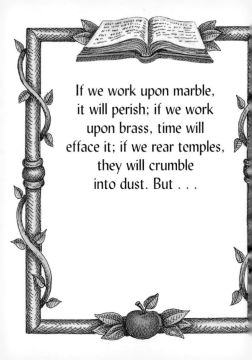

If we work upon marble,
it will perish; if we work
upon brass, time will
efface it; if we rear temples,
they will crumble
into dust. But . . .

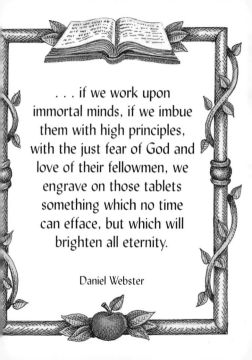

. . . if we work upon immortal minds, if we imbue them with high principles, with the just fear of God and love of their fellowmen, we engrave on those tablets something which no time can efface, but which will brighten all eternity.

Daniel Webster

Many receive instruction,
but only the wise
learn from it.

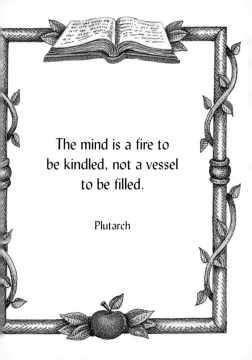

The mind is a fire to
be kindled, not a vessel
to be filled.

Plutarch

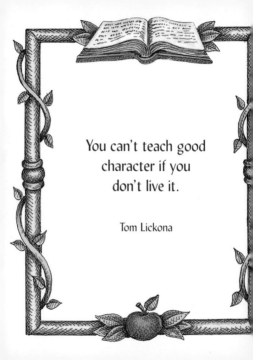

You can't teach good
character if you
don't live it.

Tom Lickona

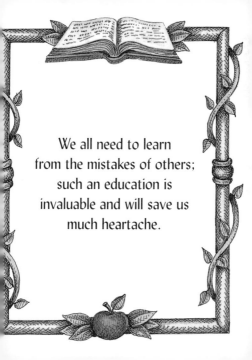

We all need to learn
from the mistakes of others;
such an education is
invaluable and will save us
much heartache.

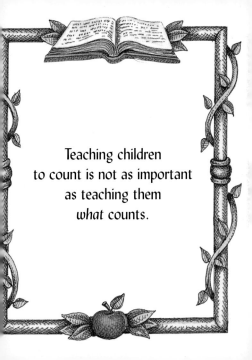

Teaching children
to count is not as important
as teaching them
what counts.

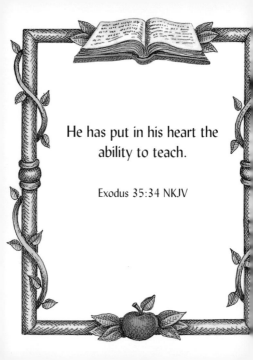

He has put in his heart the ability to teach.

Exodus 35:34 NKJV

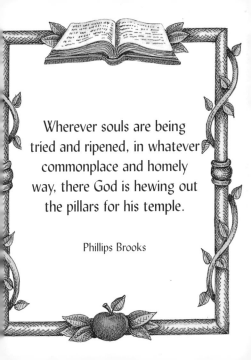

Wherever souls are being tried and ripened, in whatever commonplace and homely way, there God is hewing out the pillars for his temple.

Phillips Brooks

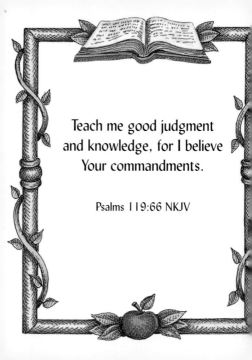

Teach me good judgment
and knowledge, for I believe
Your commandments.

Psalms 119:66 NKJV

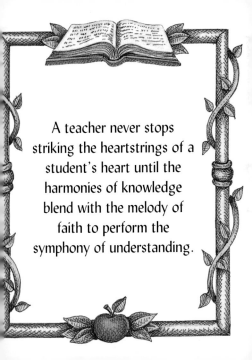

A teacher never stops striking the heartstrings of a student's heart until the harmonies of knowledge blend with the melody of faith to perform the symphony of understanding.

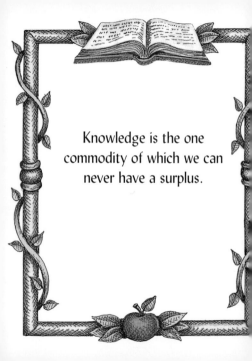

Knowledge is the one commodity of which we can never have a surplus.

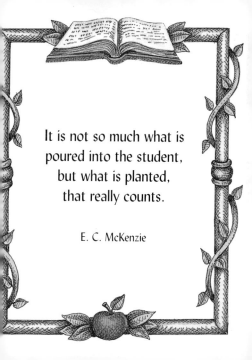

It is not so much what is
poured into the student,
but what is planted,
that really counts.

E. C. McKenzie

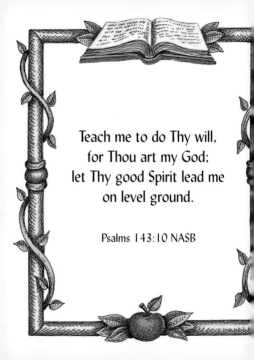

Teach me to do Thy will,
for Thou art my God;
let Thy good Spirit lead me
on level ground.

Psalms 143:10 NASB

The only thing more expensive than a good teacher is the price a community pays for an ineffective one.

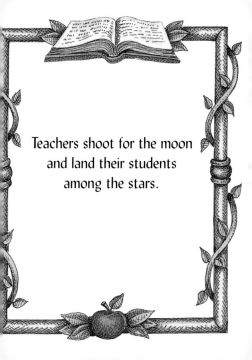

Teachers shoot for the moon
and land their students
among the stars.

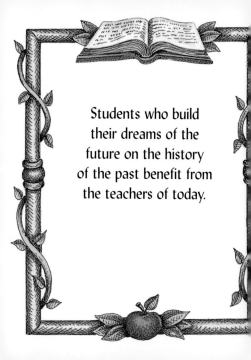

Students who build
their dreams of the
future on the history
of the past benefit from
the teachers of today.

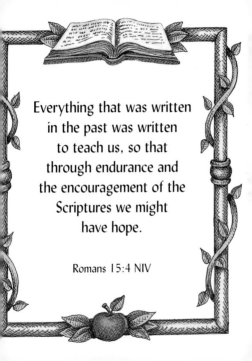

Everything that was written
in the past was written
to teach us, so that
through endurance and
the encouragement of the
Scriptures we might
have hope.

Romans 15:4 NIV

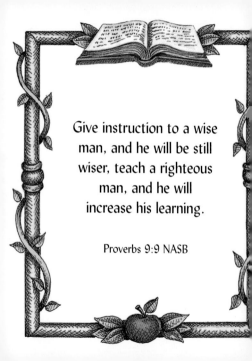

Give instruction to a wise man, and he will be still wiser, teach a righteous man, and he will increase his learning.

Proverbs 9:9 NASB

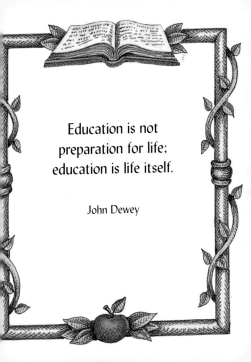

Education is not
preparation for life;
education is life itself.

John Dewey

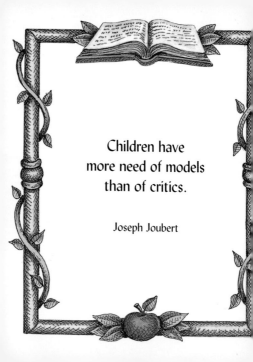

Children have
more need of models
than of critics.

Joseph Joubert

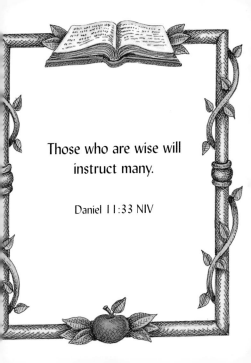

Those who are wise will instruct many.

Daniel 11:33 NIV

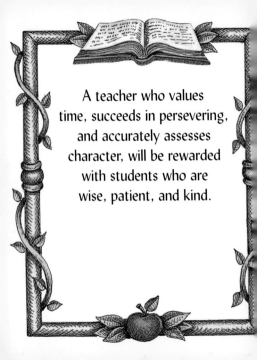

A teacher who values
time, succeeds in persevering,
and accurately assesses
character, will be rewarded
with students who are
wise, patient, and kind.

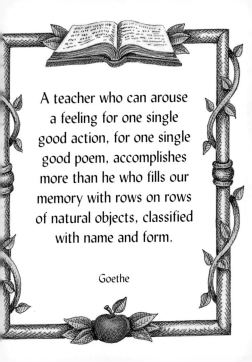

A teacher who can arouse
a feeling for one single
good action, for one single
good poem, accomplishes
more than he who fills our
memory with rows on rows
of natural objects, classified
with name and form.

Goethe

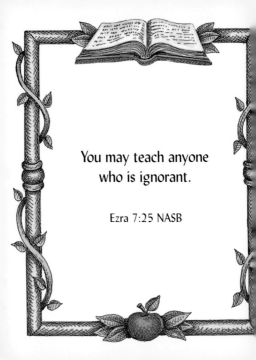

You may teach anyone
who is ignorant.

Ezra 7:25 NASB

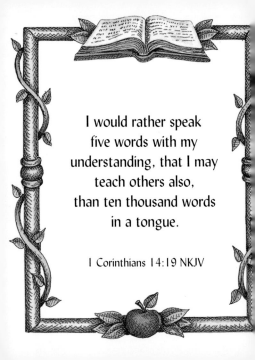

I would rather speak
five words with my
understanding, that I may
teach others also,
than ten thousand words
in a tongue.

1 Corinthians 14:19 NKJV

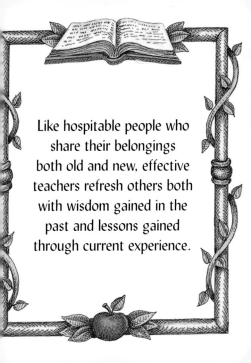

Like hospitable people who share their belongings both old and new, effective teachers refresh others both with wisdom gained in the past and lessons gained through current experience.

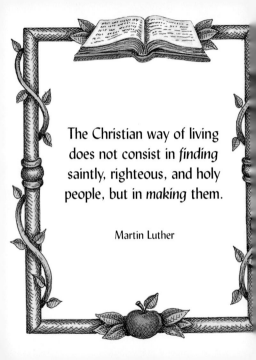

The Christian way of living does not consist in *finding* saintly, righteous, and holy people, but in *making* them.

Martin Luther

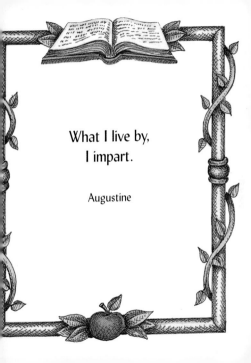

What I live by,
I impart.

Augustine

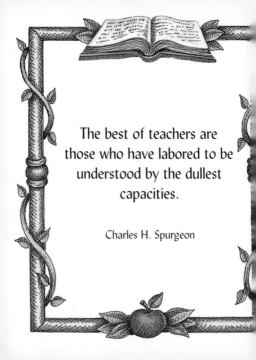

The best of teachers are those who have labored to be understood by the dullest capacities.

Charles H. Spurgeon

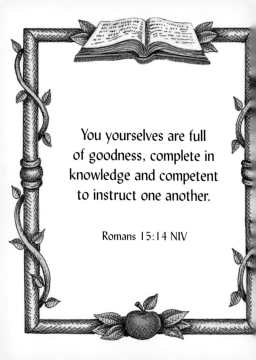

You yourselves are full of goodness, complete in knowledge and competent to instruct one another.

Romans 15:14 NIV

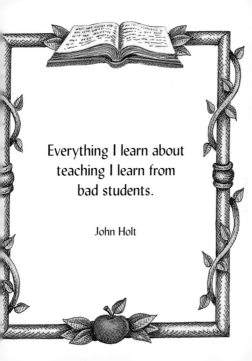

Everything I learn about
teaching I learn from
bad students.

John Holt

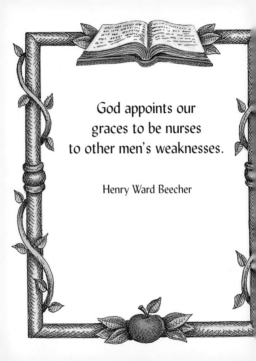

God appoints our
graces to be nurses
to other men's weaknesses.

Henry Ward Beecher

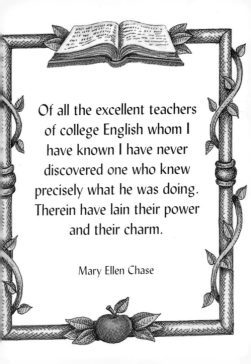

Of all the excellent teachers of college English whom I have known I have never discovered one who knew precisely what he was doing. Therein have lain their power and their charm.

Mary Ellen Chase

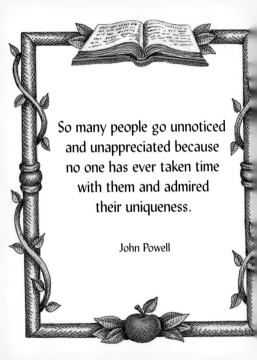

So many people go unnoticed
and unappreciated because
no one has ever taken time
with them and admired
their uniqueness.

John Powell

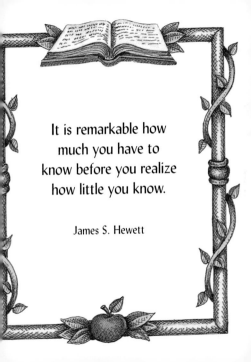

It is remarkable how
much you have to
know before you realize
how little you know.

James S. Hewett

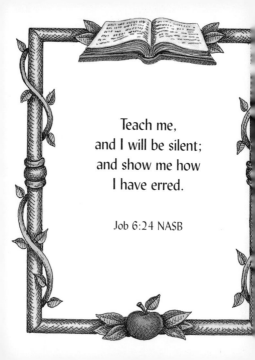

Teach me,
and I will be silent;
and show me how
I have erred.

Job 6:24 NASB

A man who has never gone to school may steal from a freight car; but if he has a university education, he may steal the whole railroad.

Theodore Roosevelt

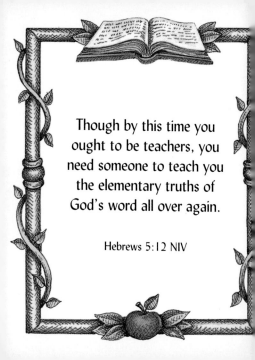

Though by this time you ought to be teachers, you need someone to teach you the elementary truths of God's word all over again.

Hebrews 5:12 NIV

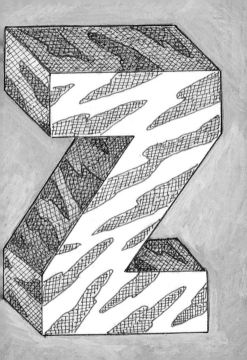

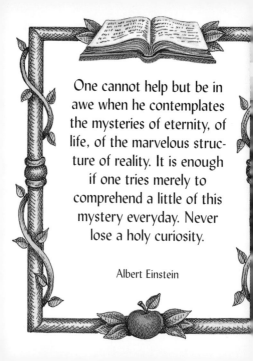

One cannot help but be in awe when he contemplates the mysteries of eternity, of life, of the marvelous structure of reality. It is enough if one tries merely to comprehend a little of this mystery everyday. Never lose a holy curiosity.

Albert Einstein

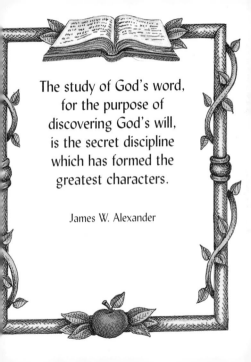

The study of God's word,
for the purpose of
discovering God's will,
is the secret discipline
which has formed the
greatest characters.

James W. Alexander

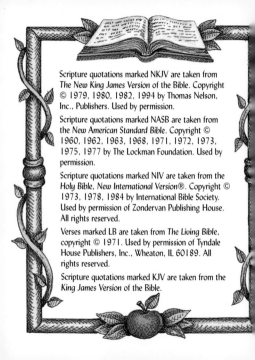